PSALMS
FOR
FEASTS
AND
SEASONS

PSALMS
FOR
FEASTS
AND
SEASONS

Revised and Augmented Full Music Edition

CHRISTOPHER WILLCOCK

COLLINS DOVE
Melbourne Australia

Published by Collins Dove
25-37 Huntingdale Road
Burwood Victoria 3125
Telephone (03) 805 1777

First published 1977, this revised edition 1990
Designed and Illustrated by John Canty
Typeset in Times by Musictype Pty. Ltd.
Printed in Australia by Globe Press Pty. Ltd.

The National Library of Australia
Cataloguing-in-Publication Data:
Willcock, Christopher.
Psalms for feasts & seasons.

ISBN 0 85924 841 0.

1. Psalms (Music).2. Church year.I.Title.

782.5294172

CONTENTS

Introduction
Psalm Tables

COMMON RESPONSORIAL PSALMS

COMMON RESPONSES

denotes page turns

INTRODUCTION

The psalms are at once prayer and song. The various attitudes of prayer : praise, petition, thanksgiving, have always been recognized in the psalms. That they are *lyrical* texts and enjoy only half-lives if they are merely recited has been less well-understood. The growing use of psalms as sung vehicles of prayer is a very welcome rediscovery.

What is offered in this collection are musical versions of the twenty-two Common Responsorial Psalms and the ten Common Responses that are gathered together in the Lectionary.

Why Common Responsorial Psalms?   The Lectionary offers the Common Responsorial Psalms and Common Responses as a resource for communities who wish to sing the responsorial psalm, but whose musical capabilities would prevent them from singing the psalm proper to every Sunday and major feast. These proper psalms change at each celebration. A psalm chosen from the common collection may therefore be used if the responsorial psalm that follows the first reading on a particular day is not known in a musical setting. The General Instruction of the Roman Missal (4th edition, 1975), no. 36, indicates the pastoral use of the Common Responsorial Psalms and that of the Common Responses: "In order that the people may be able to join in the responsorial psalm more readily, some texts of responses and psalms have been chosen, according to different seasons of the year and classes of saints, for optional use, whenever the psalm is sung, in place of the text corresponding to the reading."

The common psalms are arranged in two sections: the first providing texts for the major feasts and seasons of the church's year; the second, psalms that are not specified liturgically. Psalms from the first section may, of course, be used outside the major feasts and seasons. The criterion governing all usage is that the psalm be related in some degree to the reading that precedes it. As a help in choosing an appropriate psalm, thematic and liturgical indications are included in the suggestions given at the head of each psalm setting.

By using this varied group of psalms and responses a particular community can gradually build up its repertoire. As new psalms are learnt, the changes can be rung with greater interest. This relieves music directors and congregations of the problem of either coping with many new psalms in rapid succession, or using a few psalms that are well-known but do not properly fulfil their function after a given first reading.

Resources   The simplest forces are envisaged: a cantor to introduce the Antiphon and then sing the psalm verses; an assembly to respond to the texts of the psalms by using the Antiphon; and a keyboard player to provide the accompaniment. Chord symbols are provided for guitarists and keyboard players. Further performance possibilities are suggested in the Performance Notes at the end of the book.

Psalm Tables   Communities do not all have the same needs, resources or experience in psalmody, and the frequency at which a sung psalm can be changed will vary from one community to another. Some may be able to choose a different Common Responsorial Psalm for each celebration, others, however, may judge it more pastorally effective if the same psalm is used over a number of consecutive Sundays. Between these limits many variations are possible. To respond to the most likely situations, a set of tables has been prepared to facilitate the choice of an appropriate Common Responsorial Psalm for a particular Sunday or feast.

The *first* table lists the major feasts and seasons and suggests a Common Responsorial Psalm for each year of the three-year cycle: Years A, B and C. The *second* table lists the Sundays in Ordinary Time and suggests a Common

Responsorial Psalm for Years A, B and C. The *third* table is similar to the second but the rate of change is less frequent and a new psalm occurs only after every second, third or fourth Sunday.

A difficulty that will affect users of the third table arises from the break in the cycle of thirty-four Sundays that is caused by the movable nature of the Lenten/Easter period. The interval between the end of the Christmas season and the beginning of Lent can be as short as six Sundays of Ordinary Time and as many as nine. This variability will obviously affect any programme that sets down a pattern of psalm grouping for consecutive Sundays. Every year the pattern will be broken at some point between the seventh and the twelfth Sundays of Ordinary Time.

Common Responses   Another method whereby a community may always be able to sing the psalm and not have to learn a new Antiphon every time is by using the Common Responses. These ten settings, distributed between the liturgical seasons and the two general categories of praise and petition, may be attached to any appropriate psalm whose verses a cantor sings using the psalm tone provided. A number of sample psalm verses have been included here to demonstrate the procedure. Once they are accustomed to the practice, cantors will normally be able to use the psalm verses that the Lectionary provides for each Liturgy of the Word.

A further use for the Easter Common Response: "Alleluia", should be mentioned. This Response and its accompanying psalm Tone could well be used for the Gospel Acclamation outside Lent.

Other uses   The Psalms and Responses may also be found useful at times other than during the Liturgy of the Word. Opportunities will present themselves at other points in the celebration of the Eucharist. Furthermore, communities praying the Liturgy of the Hours may find these settings of use for the singing of the psalms.

Any attention given to the expressive delivery of the words of the psalms that is allied to a care over musical phrasing and rhythm will be amply repaid in the prayerful response that the whole community brings to receiving God's word.

Christopher Willcock S.J.
Melbourne, 1989

PSALM TABLES

TABLE 1: SEASONS AND FEASTS

Sunday or Feast	Suggested Common Psalm		
	Year A	Year B	Year C
Advent 1	122	130	25
Advent 2	72	85	85
Advent 3	25	27	145
Advent 4	85	91	85
Christmas Midnight Mass	98	98	98
Christmas Mass at Dawn	98	98	98
Christmas Mass during the Day	98	98	98
Holy Family	19	19	19
Mary, Mother of God	145	145	145
Epiphany	72	72	72
Baptism of the Lord	72	72	72
Ash Wednesday	51	51	51
Lent 1	51	25	91
Lent 2	145	95	27
Lent 3	95	19	103
Lent 4	72	130	34
Lent 5	130	51	27
Passion Sunday	22	22	22
Holy Thursday	34	34	34
Good Friday	22	22	22
Easter Vigil: 1	104	104	104
Easter Vigil: 2	25	25	25
Easter Vigil: 3	136	136	136
Easter Vigil: 4	103	103	103
Easter Vigil: 5	63	63	63
Easter Vigil: 6	19	19	19
Easter Vigil: 7	51	51	51
Easter Vigil: 8	118	118	118
Easter 1	118	118	118
Easter 2	118	118	118
Easter 3	118	118	118
Easter 4	63	118	100
Easter 5	100	145	145
Easter 6	66	98	27
Ascension	47	47	47
Easter 7	27	103	130
Pentecost	104	104	104
Trinity	145	103	145
Corpus Christi	34	34	34
Sacred Heart	103	63	100

TABLE 2: SUNDAYS IN ORDINARY TIME
Psalms changing each Sunday

Sunday	Suggested Common Psalm		
	Year A	Year B	Year C
2	98	122	98
3	27	25	19
4	85	95	85
5	27	63	27
6	19	130	85
7	103	51	103
8	63	103	19
9	63	19	122
10	51	130	130
11	100	104	51
12	25	136	63
13	91	103	25
14	145	95	66
15	104	85	19
16	130	100	34
17	19	145	103
18	145	104	95
19	85	34	100
20	27	34	25
21	100	34	66
22	63	19	91
23	95	98	19
24	103	91	51
25	145	130	25
26	25	19	85
27	34	19	95
28	34	27	98
29	98	22	130
30	103	91	34
31	95	103	145
32	63	100	118
33	25	25	98
34	100	72	122

TABLE 3: SUNDAYS IN ORDINARY TIME
Psalms changing less frequently

Sunday	Suggested Common Psalm		
	Year A	Year B	Year C
2	27	95	100
3	27	95	100
4	27	95	27
5	27	51	27
6	19	51	27
7	19	51	103
8	19	130	103
9	19	130	103
10	25	130	130
11	25	103	130
12	25	103	63
13	25	103	63
14	145	103	63
15	145	85	19
16	145	85	19
17	85	85	19
18	85	85	95
19	85	34	95
20	100	34	95
21	100	34	95
22	63	19	85
23	63	19	85
24	103	91	51
25	103	91	51
26	103	27	51
27	34	27	25
28	34	27	25
29	95	63	145
30	95	63	145
31	95	63	145
32	122	122	122
33	122	122	122
34	122	122	122

The horizontal lines indicate when a psalm changes within an annual cycle.

COMMON
RESPONSORIAL
PSALMS

O YOU, O LORD

USE: *Advent; penance; First Friends; anointing of the sick; instruction and discipleship; God's guidance*

ANTIPHON *Moderately*

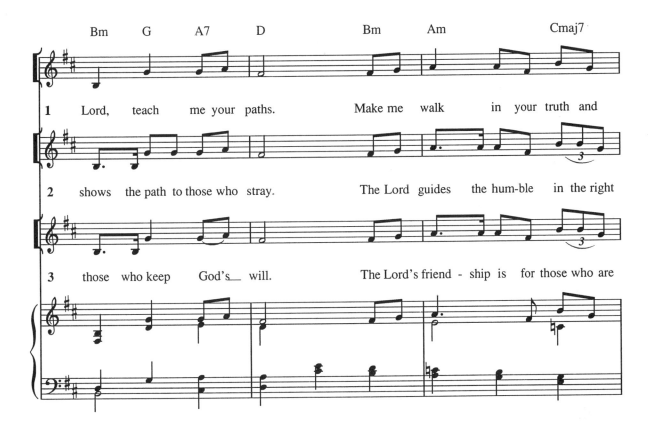

Bm   G   A7   D   Bm   Am   Cmaj7

1   Lord,   teach   me your   paths.   Make me   walk   in   your   truth and

2   shows   the path to those who   stray.   The Lord   guides   the hum-ble   in the right

3   those   who keep   God's   will.   The Lord's friend - ship is   for those who are

Am   Dm/F   Em7/G   A   F♯m   Bm

Antiphon

1   teach   me: for   you   are   God_____ my_____ sa-viour.

Antiphon

2   path,   and   teach-es God's way_____ to   the   poor.

Antiphon

3   faith-ful,   to   them God's love   has   been   re - vealed.

Antiphon

3

LORD, LET US SEE YOUR KINDNESS

USE: *Advent; promise; harmony and peace; justice*

ANTIPHON *At a measured pace*

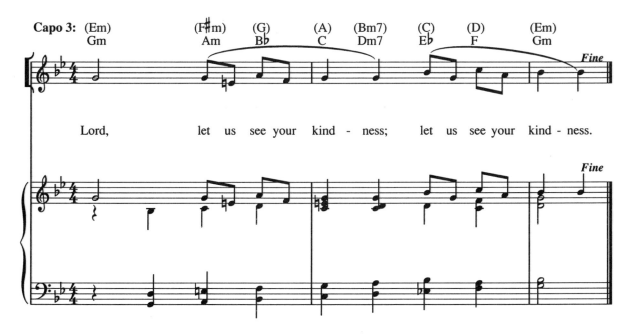

Lord, let us see your kind - ness; let us see your kind - ness.

Cantor (to be sung before verse 1 only)

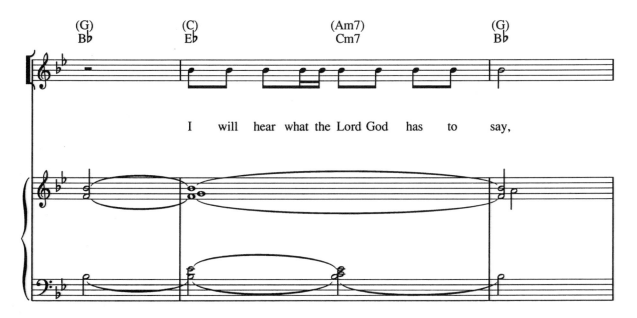

I will hear what the Lord God has to say,

VERSES

1 a voice___ that speaks_ of___ peace, peace_ for God's peo - ple and friends. Sal-

2 For mer-cy and faith-ful-ness have met; jus - tice and peace_ have em-braced.

3 The Lord___ will make_ us___ pros-per and our earth shall yield___ its___ fruit.

1 va - tion is near for those who fear God, whose glo - ry will dwell in our land. *Antiphon*

2 Faith-ful-ness shall spring from the earth___ and_ jus - tice shall look down from heaven.___ *Antiphon*

3 Jus - tice shall march be-fore the Lord___ and_ peace shall fol-low God's steps. *Antiphon*

ALL THE ENDS OF THE EARTH

USE: *Christmas; religious profession; ordination; spread of the gospel; praise*

ANTIPHON 1 *Brightly*

All the ends of the earth have seen___ the sa - ving pow'r of God.___

have seen

ANTIPHON 2 *Brightly*

Sing a new song to the Lord, the work-er of won-ders.

God_ will rule_ the world with jus - tice_ and the peo-ples with fair - ness.

VERSES

1. Sing a new song to the Lord, the work-er of won-ders God's right hand and arm have brought sal-va-tion. *Antiphon*
2. The Lord has made the vic-t'ry known and jus-tice to na-tions. God has re-mem-bered a mer-ci-ful love for the house of Is-ra-el. *Antiphon*
3. All the ends of earth have seen our God's sal-va-tion. O shout to the Lord all the earth, ring out your glad-ness. *Antiphon*
4. Sing psalms to the Lord with the sound of the harp, with the sound of mu-sic. With trum-pets and sound of the horn, ac-claim the king, the Lord. *Antiphon*

7

VERSE 5

Let the sea and all with-in it thun-der; the world and all its peo-ples. Let the ri-vers clap their hands and the

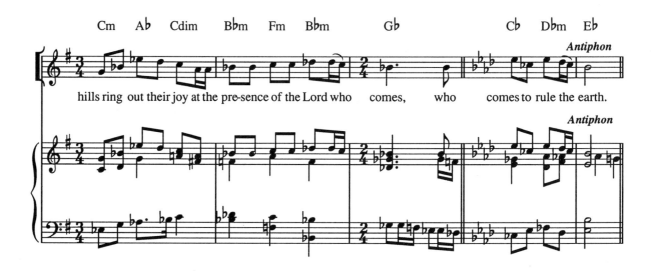

hills ring out their joy at the pre-sence of the Lord who comes, who comes to rule the earth.

Antiphon

ANTIPHON 1

All the ends of the earth have seen____ the sa-ving pow'r of God.____
have seen

Fine

8

ANTIPHON 2

Sing a new song to the Lord, the work-er of won - ders. God will rule the

Sing a new song to the Lord, the work-er of won-ders. God will rule the world with

world with jus - tice and with fair - ness.

jus - tice and the peo-ples with fair - ness.

LORD, EVERY NATION

USE: *Epiphany; peace and justice*

ANTIPHON *With a steady tread*

VERSES 1, 2, 4

1   O God,   give your judge-ment to the king,   to a

2   In his days   jus - tice shall flour-ish   and

4   For he shall save the   poor__ when they   cry   and the

11

VERSE 3

BE MERCIFUL, O LORD

USE: *Lent; penance; initiation; recognition of mercy*

ANTIPHON *Slow, with gentle pulse*

Be mer-ci-ful, O Lord, for we have sinned; be mer-ci-ful, O Lord for we have sinned.

VERSES

1 Have mer-cy on me, God, in your kind-ness. In your com-pas-sion blot out my of-fence.

2 My of - fen-ces tru - ly I know them; my__ sin is al - ways be - fore me.

3 A pure heart cre-ate for me, O God, put a stead - fast spi - rit with - in me.

4 Give me a-gain the joy of your help; with a spi-rit of fer-vour sus-tain me.

1 O__ wash me more and more from my guilt and. cleanse me from my sin.

2 A-gainst you, you a - lone, have I sinned; what is e - vil in your sight I have done.

3 Do not cast me a - way from your pres-ence, nor de-prive me of your ho - ly spir-it.

4 O__ Lord, o - pen my lips, and my mouth shall de - clare your praise.

15

BE WITH ME, LORD

USE: *Lent; God's protection*

ANTIPHON *With steady, forward movement*

Be with me Lord, be with me, Lord, when___ I am in trou-ble.

VERSES

1 You who dwell in the sha-dow of the Most High and a-

2 U-pon you no e-vil shall fall, no___

3 They shall bear you u-pon their___ hands lest you

4 "Since they cling to me in love, I will free them; pro-

1 bide in the shade of the Al-migh-ty say to the Lord: "My

2 plague ap-proach where you dwell. For you has God com-man - ded the

3 strike your foot a-gainst a stone. On the lion and the vi-per you will

4 tect them for they know my name. When they call I shall ans-wer: 'I am

1 re - fuge, my strong - hold, my God in whom I trust!"

2 an - gels to keep you in all your ways.

3 tread and tram - ple the young lion and the dra-gon.

4 with you.' I will save them in dis - tress and give them glo-ry."

Antiphon

17

ITH THE LORD THERE IS MERCY

USE: *Lent; penance; repentance and trust; funerals and Masses for the dead*

PSALM *130*

MY GOD, MY GOD

USE: *Holy Week; lament; trial and ordeal*

ANTIPHON *Slow and expressive*

My God, my God, why have you a - ban - doned me?

1. All who see me de - ride me, They curl their lips, they
2. Ma - ny dogs have sur - round - ed me, a wick - ed band be -
3. They di - vide my clothes a - mong them. They cast lots for my
4. I will tell your name to my peo - ple and praise you where they

21

GOD'S LOVE IS EVERLASTING

USE: *Easter Vigil; litany of praise history of salvation*

PSALM *136*

23

24

HIS IS THE DAY

USE: *Easter, Christian unity; praise*

PSALM *118*

ANTIPHON *Brightly*

This is the day the Lord has made; let us re-joice and be glad.

This is the day the Lord has made; let us re-joice and be glad.

Fine

VERSES

1 Give thanks for the Lord is good, for God's love en-dures for

2 The Lord's right hand has tri-umphed; God's right hand raised me

3 The stone which the build-ers re - jec - ted has be - come the cor - ner -

27

LET ALL THE EARTH

USE: *Easter; Initiation; communal thanksgiving*

PSALM 66

ANTIPHON *Strongly*

Let all the earth cry out to God with joy: Alleluia; cry out: Alleluia!

VERSE 1 Cry out with joy to God, all the earth, O sing to the glory of God's name. O

28

give voice to glor - ious praise. Say to God: "How tre-men-dous your deeds."

VERSE 2,3,4

2 Be - fore you all the earth shall bow, shall

3 God___ turned the sea in - to dry land; they

4 Come and hear, all who fear___ God. I will

29

30

![G]OD MOUNTS THE THRONE

USE: *Ascension; praise and gladness*

PSALM 47

ANTIPHON *With well-marked, steady accents*

God mounts the throne to shouts of joy, to shouts of joy, joy.

VERSES

1. All___ peo-ples, clap your hands, cry to

2. God goes up with shouts of joy: the Lord goes

3. God is king of all the earth, sing___

1   God   with shouts of joy!   For the Lord,   the Most High,   we re-

2   up   with trum-pet blast.   Sing praise   for God,   sing

3   praise   with all your skill.   God is king   o - ver all   the

1   vere,   great king   o - ver all   the earth.   *Antiphon*

2   praise,   sing praise   to our king,   sing praise.   *Antiphon*

3   na - tions;   God reigns   on the ho - ly   throne.   *Antiphon*

LORD, SEND OUT YOUR SPIRIT

USE: *Pentecost; confirmation;
creation*

PSALM *104*

ANTIPHON *With a flowing pulse*

Lord, send out your Spi - rit, and re - new the face of___ the earth.

VERSE 1

Cantor

O bless the Lord, my soul; Lord__ God, how great__ you are! How

34

VERSE 2

VERSE 3

36

ANTIPHON (last time)

LORD, YOU HAVE THE WORDS

USE: *General; God's word and law;*
Institution of Readers

PSALM *19*

ANTIPHON *Smoothly*

1 it re-vives the soul. The rule of the Lord is to be

2 glad - den the heart. The com-mand of the Lord___ is___

3 bi - ding for e - ver. The de - crees of the Lord___ are___

4 pur - est of gold, and sweet-er are they___ than___

1 trus-ted, it gives wis-dom to the sim-ple.

2 clear, it gives light___ to the eyes.

3 truth, and all of them are just.

4 hon - ey, than hon - ey from the comb.

HE LORD IS MY LIGHT

USE: *General; Marriages; Baptisms; Funerals; Religious profession; Ordination*

PSALM 27

ANTIPHON 1 *With a gentle movement*

ANTIPHON 2 *Unhurried*

mine; I have called you by_ your name, you are mine.

VERSE 1

The Lord is my light and my help; whom shall I fear? The

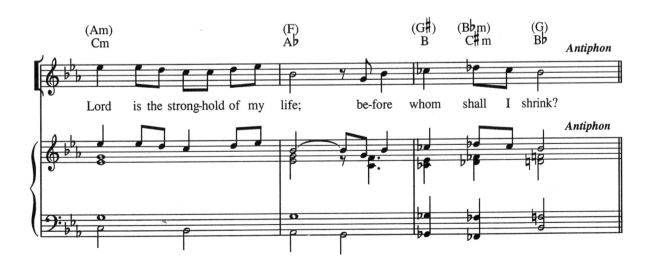

Lord is the strong-hold of my life; be-fore whom shall I shrink?

Antiphon

Antiphon

VERSE 2

There is one thing I ask of the Lord, for this I long: to

Ah

live in the house of the Lord all the days of my life.

Antiphon

42

VERSE 3
(A) C (C♯) E (C) E♭ (G♯) B
S A T B
I am sure I shall see the Lord's good - ness in the land of the
(C) E♭ (Am) Cm (F) A♭ (Em7) Gm7 (G♯) B (B♭m7) D♭m7 (G) B♭
liv - ing. Hope in God, hold_ firm and take heart, hope in the Lord.
Antiphon
Antiphon

ANTIPHON 2

Do not be a-fraid I am with you; I have called you by your name, you are mine; I have

called you by your name, you are mine.

TASTE AND SEE

USE: *General; Praise and reverence;*
Eucharist; Initiation; Baptism;
Religious profession; Anointing;
Marriage

PSALM 34

ANTIPHON *With flowing movement*

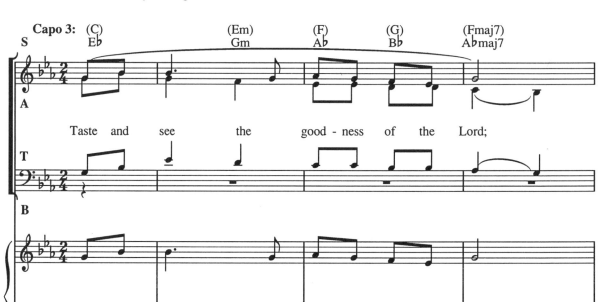

Taste and see the good-ness of the Lord;

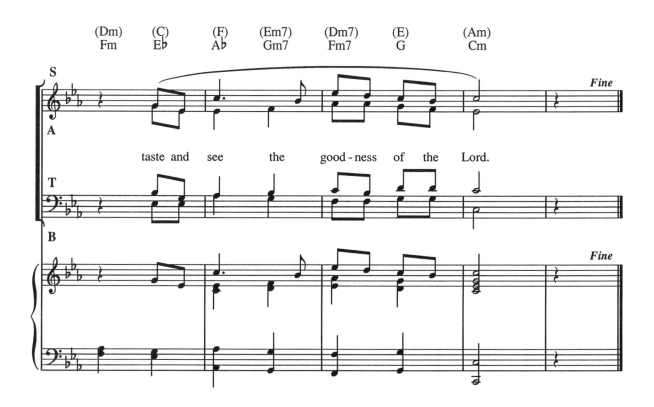

taste and see the good-ness of the Lord.

VERSES

47

MY SOUL IS THIRSTING

USE: *General; Initiation;*
Communion; desire and longing;
reliance on God; Religious
profession; Funerals

PSALM 63

ANTIPHON *Smoothly*

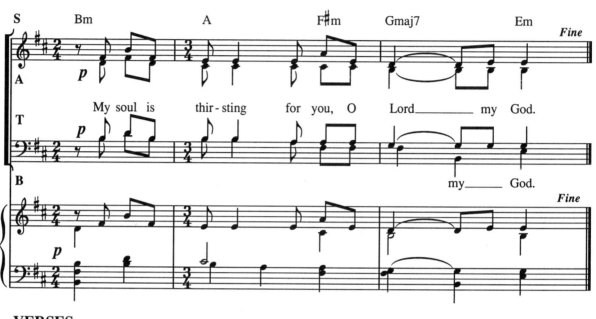

My soul is thir-sting for you, O Lord_____ my God.

my_____ God.

VERSES

1. O God, my God, for you I long for
2. So I gaze on you in your dwell-ing to
3. So I will bless you all my life, in your
4. For_____ you have been my help; in your

48

IF TODAY YOU HEAR GOD'S VOICE

USE: *General; Invitatory;*
response to God's word; Penance

PSALM *95*

ANTIPHON *Brightly and with movement*

VERSE 1

50

VERSE 2

VERSE 3

WE ARE GOD'S PEOPLE

USE: *General; entrance rite;*
community; Religious profession;
Ordination; Christian unity

PSALM *100*

INTRODUCTION *Steady tempo throughout*

VERSES

1. Cry out with joy to the Lord all the earth. Serve_____ the Lord with

2. Know that the Lord_____ is_____ God who made us,_ to whom we be-

3. Go in the tem-ple gates gi-ving thanks. En-ter the courts with songs. of

4. See then how good_____ is the Lord, whose love is e-ter-nal-ly

1 glad-ness. Come be-fore God sing-ing for joy.

2 long, we are God's peo - ple the sheep of the flock.

3 praise. Give thanks to God and bless the Lord's name.

4 strong. God is faith - ful from age___ to age.

ANTIPHON (last time)

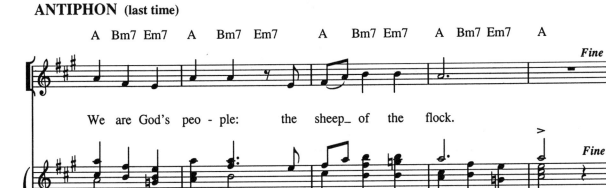

We are God's peo - ple: the sheep_ of the flock.

THE LORD IS KIND AND MERCIFUL

PSALM *103*

ANTIPHON *Expressively*

1 be - ing, bless God's ho - ly name. My___ soul, give thanks to the

2 heals___ all your ills, who re - deems your life from the

3 an - ger, rich in mer - cy, treats us not ac - cor - ding to

4 far does God re - move our sins. As a fa - ther has re - gard for his

1 Lord and ne - ver for - get all your bless-ings. *Antiphon*

2 grave, who crowns you with love and com - pas-sion. *Antiphon*

3 sin nor re - pays us ac - cor - ding to our faults. *Antiphon*

4 sons, the Lord will for - give those who are faith-ful. *Antiphon*

I WILL PRAISE YOUR NAME

USE: *General; Confirmation;*
thanksgiving; Marriage;
Institution of Acolytes; Eucharist;
God's grandeur

PSALM *145*

ANTIPHON *Brightly*

LET US GO REJOICING

USE: *General; entrance; funerals; peace and justice; Christian unity; homecoming; pilgrimage*

PSALM *122*

ANTIPHON *March-like*

60

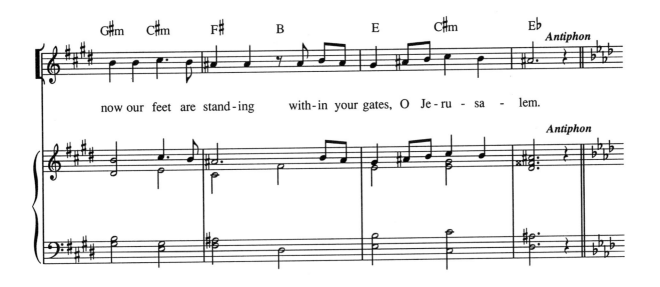

now our feet are stand-ing with-in your gates, O Je-ru - sa - lem.

VERSES 2, 3, 4, 5

2   Je - ru-sa-lem is built as a ci - ty   strong - ly com-pact._____   It is

3   For   Is - rael's law   it   is   there to praise the Lord's name._____

4   For the peace of Je-ru-sa-lem   pray: "Peace be to your homes!_____   May

5   For the love of my fa-m'ly and friends   I say:"Peace be u-pon   you!"___   For the

2   there   that the tribes go   up,   the_ tribes   of the   Lord.

3   There were set the thrones of   judge-ment   of the house   of___   Da-vid.

4   peace   reign   in your   walls,   in your   pal-a-ces,   peace!"

5   love   of the house of the   Lord   I will ask   for your   good.

62

COMMON
RESPONSES

OME, O LORD, AND SET US FREE

USE: *Advent*

Come, O Lord, and set us free, come, _____ O Lord. _____

TONE

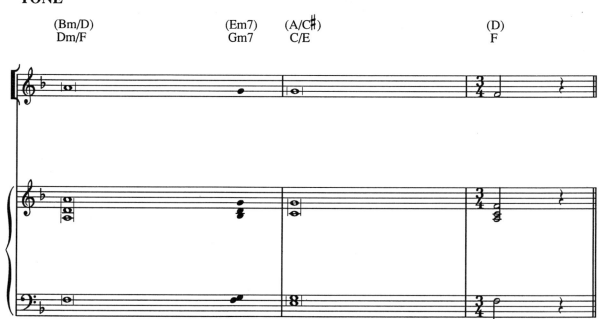

 **DVENT PSALMS**

Psalm 24

The Lord's is the earth and its *full* ness,
the world and all its p<u>eo</u>ples.
It is the Lord who set it on the *seas*;
and made it firm on the <u>wa</u>ters.
 Response
Who shall climb the mountain of the *Lord*?
Who shall stand in God's holy <u>place</u>?
Those with clean hands and pure *heart*,
who desire not worthless <u>things</u>.
 Response
They shall receive blessings from the *Lord*
and reward from the God who <u>saves</u> them.
These are the ones who seek the *Lord*,
seek the face of the God of <u>Ja</u>cob.
 Response

Psalm 80

O Lord, rouse up your *might*,
O Lord, come to our <u>help</u>.
 Response
God of hosts bring us *back*;
let your face shine on us and we shall be <u>saved</u>.
 Response
You brought a vine out of *E* gypt;
to plant it you drove out the <u>na</u>tions.
Before it you cleared the *ground*;
it took root and spread through the <u>land</u>.
 Response
God of hosts, turn again, we im*plore*,
look down from heaven and <u>see</u>.
Visit your vine and pro*tect* it,
the vine your right hand has <u>pla</u>nted.
 Response

TODAY WE HAVE SEEN YOUR GLORY, O LORD

USE: *Christmas*

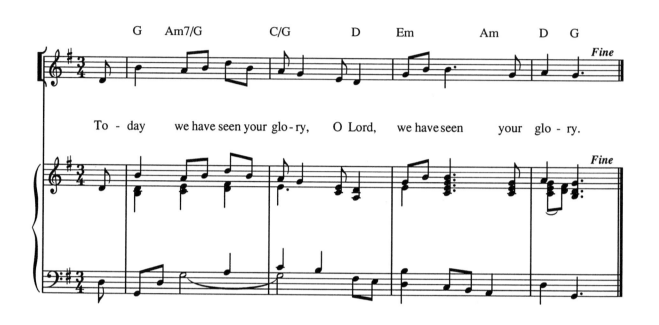

To - day we have seen your glo - ry, O Lord, we have seen your glo - ry.

TONE

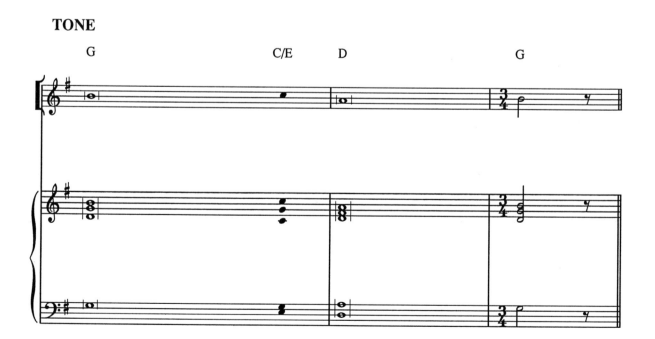

CHRISTMAS - EPIPHANY PSALMS

Psalm 96   *Christmas*

O sing a new song to the Lord,
sing to the Lord all the *earth*.
O sing to the Lord, bless God's <u>name</u>.
    Response
Proclaim the Lord's help day by *day*,
tell among the nations God's glory,
and the wonders among all the <u>peo</u>ples.
    Response
Let the heavens rejoice and earth be *glad*,
let the sea and all within it thunder <u>praise</u>.
    Response
Let the land and all it bears rejoice,
all the trees of the wood shout for *joy*
at the presence of the Lord who comes,
who comes to rule the <u>earth</u>.
    Response
With justice God will rule the *world*,
and judge the peoples with <u>truth</u>.
    Response

Psalm 72   *Epiphany*

O God, give your judgement to the *king*,
to a king's son your <u>jus</u>tice,
that he may judge your people in *jus* tice
and your poor in right <u>judge</u>ment.
    Response
In his days justice shall *flou*rish
and peace till the <u>moo</u>n fails.
He shall rule from sea to *sea*,
from the Great River to earth's <u>bounds</u>.
    Response
The kings of Tarshish and the seacoasts
shall pay him *tri*bute.
The kings of Sheba and Seba
shall bring him <u>gifts</u>.
Before him all rulers shall fall *pros* trate,
all nations shall <u>serve</u> him.
    Response
For he shall save the poor when they *cry*
and the needy who are <u>help</u>less.
He will have pity on the *weak*
and save the lives of the <u>poor</u>.
    Response

 **EMEMBER, O LORD**

USE: *Lent*

Re-mem-ber, O Lord,_ re-mem-ber, O Lord,_ re-mem-ber your faith-ful-ness and love.

TONE

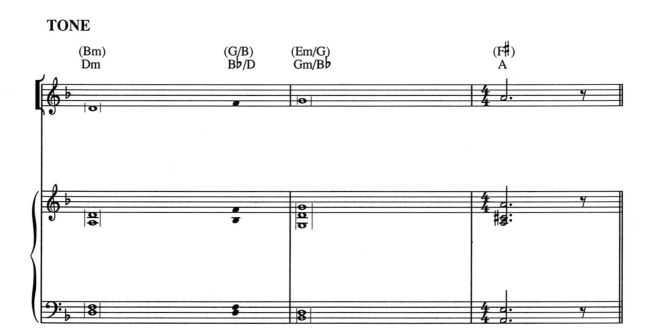

LENTEN PSALMS

Psalm 51

Have mercy on me, God, in your *kind*ness.
In your compassion blot out my of<u>fence</u>.
O wash me more and more from my *guilt*
and cleanse me from my <u>sin</u>.
    Response

My offences truly I *know* them;
my sin is always be<u>fore</u> me.
Against you, you alone, have I *sinned*;
what is evil in your sight I have <u>done</u>.
    Response

A pure heart create for me, O *God*,
put a steadfast spirit with<u>in</u> me.
Do not cast me away from your *pre*sence,
nor deprive me of your holy <u>spi</u>rit.
    Response

Give me again the joy of your *help*;
with a spirit of fervour sus<u>tain</u> me,
that I may teach transgressors your *ways*
and sinners may return to <u>you</u>.
    Response

Psalm 130

Out of the depths I cry to you, O *Lord*,
Lord, hear my <u>voice</u>!
O let your ears be at*ten*tive
to the voice of my <u>plea</u>ding.
    Response

If you, O Lord, should mark our *guilt*,
Lord, who would sur<u>vive</u>?
But with you is found for*give* ness;
for this we re<u>vere</u> you.
    Response

My soul is waiting for the *Lord*.
I count on God's <u>word</u>.
My soul is longing for the *Lord*
more than those who watch for <u>day</u>break.
    Response

Because with the Lord there is *mer*cy
and fullness of re<u>demp</u>tion,
Israel indeed God will re*deem*
from all its i<u>ni</u>quity.
    Response

ALLELUIA, ALLELUIA, ALLELUIA

USE: *Easter*

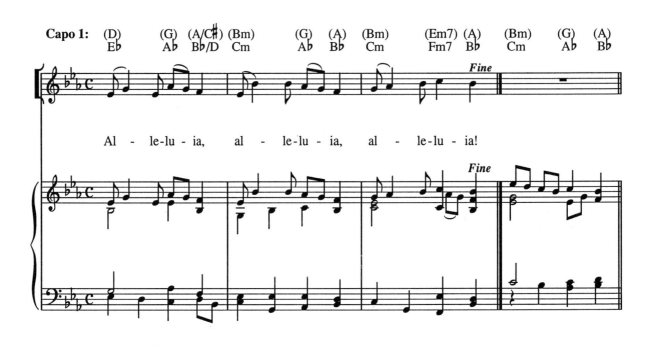

Al - le-lu - ia, al - le-lu - ia, al - le-lu - ia!

TONE

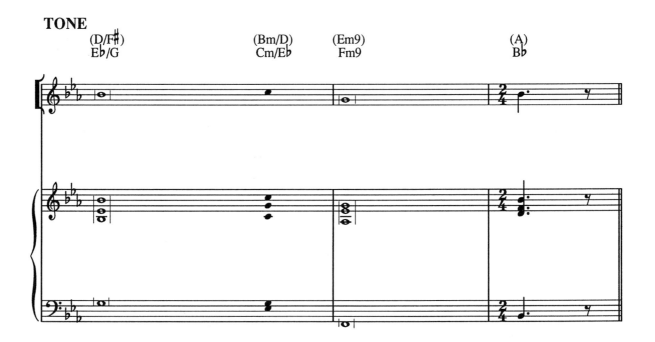

EASTER PSALMS

Psalm 118   *Easter*
Give thanks for the Lord is *good*.
God's love endures for <u>e</u>ver.
Let the tribes of Israel *say*:
"God's love endures for <u>e</u>ver."
 Response
The Lord's right hand has *tri* umphed;
God's right hand has <u>raised</u> me up.
The Lord's right hand has *tri* umphed;
I shall not die, I shall live and recount God's <u>deeds</u>.
 Response
The stone which the builders re*jec* ted
has become the <u>corner</u> stone.
This is the work of the *Lord*,
a marvel in our <u>eyes</u>.
 Response
This day was made by the *Lord*;
we rejoice and are <u>glad</u>.
 Response

Psalm 47   *Ascension*
All peoples, clap your *hands*,
cry to God with shouts of <u>joy</u>!
For the Lord, the Most High, we re*vere*,
great king over all the <u>earth</u>.
 Response
God goes up with shouts of *joy*;
the Lord goes up with trumpet <u>blast</u>.
Sing praise for God, sing *praise*,
sing praise to our king, sing <u>praise</u>.
 Response
God is king of all the *earth*,
sing praise with all your <u>skill</u>.
God is king over the *na*tions;
God reigns on the holy <u>throne</u>.
 Response

PRAISE THE LORD FOR THE LORD IS GOOD

USE: *Praise*

Praise___ the Lord for the Lord___ is good.___

TONE

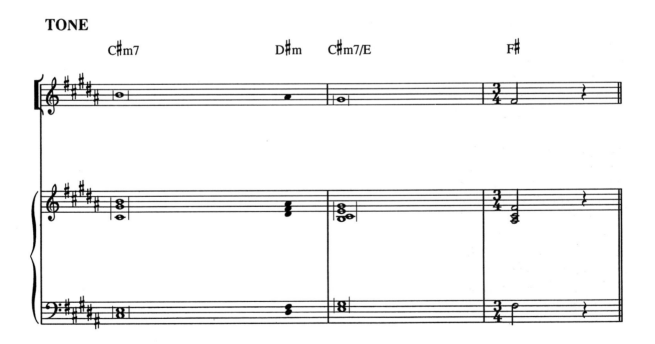

PSALM OF PRAISE 1

The goodness of the Lord

Psalm 92

It is good to give thanks to the *Lord*,
to make music to your name, O Most High,
to proclaim your love in the *mor* ning
and your truth in the watches of the night.
 Response
Your deeds, O Lord, have made me *glad*;
for the work of your hands I shout with joy.
O Lord, how great are your *works*!
How deep are your designs!
 Response
The just will flourish like the *palm* tree
and grow like a Lebanon cedar.
Planted in the house of the *Lord*
they will flourish in the courts of our God,
 Response
Still bearing fruit when they are *old*,
still full of sap, still green,
they proclaim that the Lord is *just*.
In God, my rock, there is no wrong.
 Response

Psalm 113

Praise, O servants of the *Lord*,
praise the name of the Lord!
May the name of the Lord be *blessed*
both now and for evermore!
 Response
From the rising of the sun to its *set* ting
praised be the name of the Lord!
High above the nations is the *Lord*,
above the heavens God's glory.
 Response
Who is like the Lord, our *God*,
who has risen on high to the throne
yet stoops from the heights to look *down*,
to look down upon heaven and earth?
 Response

 # WE PRAISE YOU, O LORD

USE: *Praise*

RESPONSE 6

We praise you, O Lord, for all your works are won-der-ful.

TONE

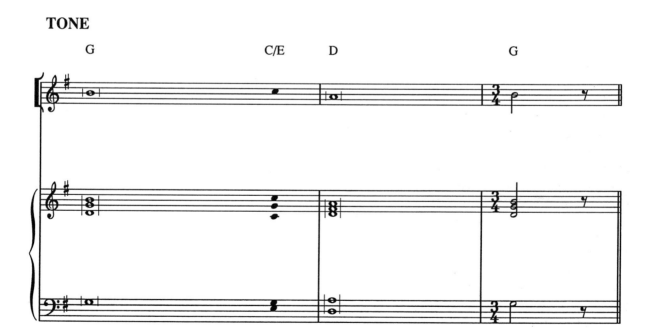

74

 **SALM OF PRAISE 2**   *God's wonderful works*

Psalm 19

The heavens proclaim your glory, O *God*,
and the firmament shows forth the work of your <u>hands</u>.
Day unto day takes up the *sto*ry
and night unto night makes known the <u>mes</u>sage.
 Response
No speech, no word, no voice is heard
yet their span extends through all the *earth*,
their words to the utmost bounds of the <u>world</u>.
 Response
There you have placed a tent for the *sun*;
it comes forth like a bridegroom coming from his tent,
rejoices like a champion to run its <u>course</u>.
 Response
At the end of the sky is the rising of the sun;
to the furthest end of the sky is its *course*.
There is nothing concealed from its burning <u>heat</u>.
 Response

Psalm 149

Sing a new song to the *Lord*,
praise God in the assembly of the <u>faith</u>ful.
Let Israel rejoice in its *ma*ker,
let Sion's people exult in their <u>king</u>.
 Response
Let the people praise God's name with *dan*cing
and the music with timbrel and <u>harp</u>.
For the Lord takes delight in the *peo*ple
and crowns the poor with sal<u>va</u>tion.
 Response
Let the faithful rejoice in their *glo*ry,
shout for joy and take their <u>rest</u>.
 Response

SING TO THE LORD A NEW SONG

USE: *Praise*

RESPONSE 7

Sing to the Lord a new song; sing to the Lord a new song.

TONE

 # SALM OF PRAISE 3

Sing a new song

Psalm 34

I will bless the Lord at all *times*,
with praise always on my l<u>ips</u>;
in the Lord my soul shall make its *boast*.
The humble shall hear and be <u>glad</u>.
    Response
Glorify the Lord with *me*.
Together let us praise God's <u>name</u>.
I sought the Lord and was *an*swered;
from my terrors God set me me <u>free</u>.
    Response
Look towards the Lord and shine in *light*;
let your faces be not a<u>shamed</u>.
When the poor cry out the Lord *hears* them
and rescues them from all their dis<u>tress</u>.
    Response
The angel of the Lord is en*camped*
around those who revere <u>God</u>.
Taste and see that the Lord is *good*.
They are happy who seek refuge in <u>God</u>.
    Response

Psalm 98

Sing a new song to the Lord,
the worker of *won*ders.
God's right hand and holy arm
have brought sal<u>va</u>tion.
    Response
The Lord has made the victory known
and power to the *na*tions.
God has remembered a merciful love
for the house of <u>Is</u>rael.
    Response
All the ends of earth have seen
our God's sal*va*tion.
O shout to the Lord all the earth,
ring out your <u>glad</u>ness.
    Response

THE LORD IS NEAR TO ALL WHO CALL

USE: *Petition*

RESPONSE 8

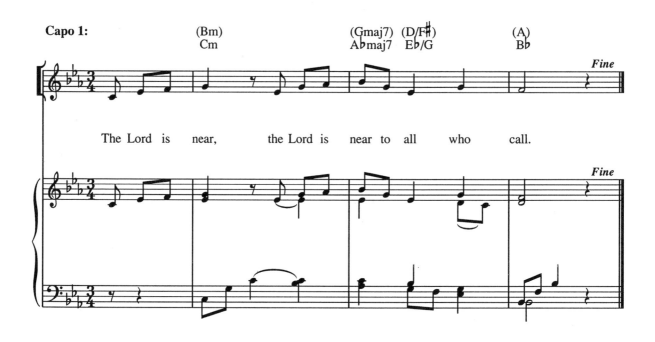

The Lord is near, the Lord is near to all who call.

TONE

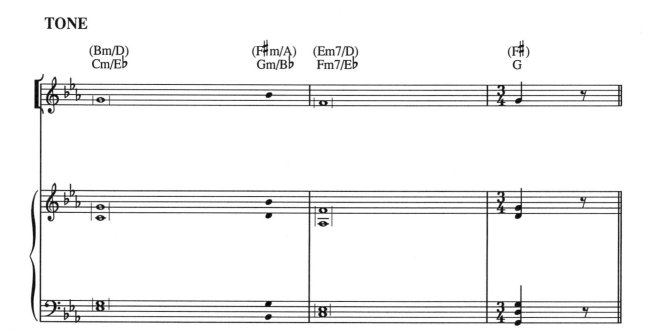

Psalm 126

When the Lord delivered Sion from *bon* dage,
it seemed like a <u>dream</u>.
Then was our mouth filled with *laugh* ter,
on our lips there were <u>songs</u>.
    Response
The heathens themselves said: "What marvels
the Lord *worked* for them!"
What marvels the Lord worked for us!
Indeed we were <u>glad</u>.
    Response
Deliver us, O Lord, from our bondage
as streams in dry *land*.
Those who are sowing in tears will sing when they <u>reap</u>.
    Response
They go out, they go out, full of tears,
carrying seed for the *sow* ing;
they come back, they come back, full of song,
carrying their <u>sheaves</u>.
    Response

Psalm 116

I trusted, even when I *said*:
"I am sorely af<u>flic</u>ted",
and when I said in my a*larm*:
"There is no one I can <u>trust</u>."
    Response
How can I repay the *Lord*
for God's goodness to <u>me</u>?
The cup of salvation I will *raise*;
I will call on the Lord's <u>name</u>.
    Response

79

HEAR US, LORD, AND SAVE US

USE: *Petition*

 RESPONSE *9*

Hear us, Lord, and save us; hear us, Lord, and save us.

TONE

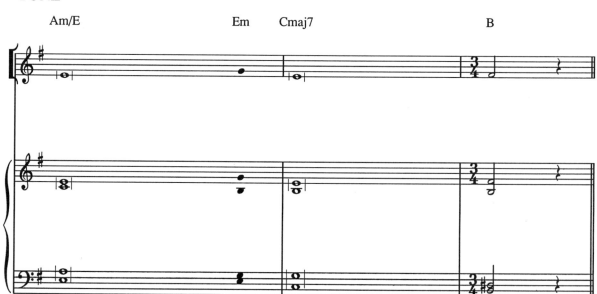

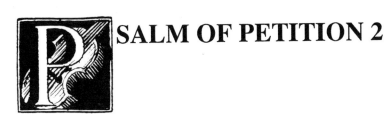

PSALM OF PETITION 2

Hear us, Lord

Psalm 43
Defend me, O God, and plead my cause
against a godless *na*tion.
From a deceitful and cunning people
rescue me, O God.
Response
O send forth your light and your *truth*;
let these be my guide.
Let them bring me to your holy *moun* tain,
to the place where you dwell.
Response
Why are you cast down, my soul,
why groan with*in* me?
Hope in God: I will praise God still,
my saviour and my God.
Response

Psalm 63
O God, my God, for you I *long*,
for you my soul is thirsting.
My body pines for *you*
like a dry weary land without water.
Response
So I gaze on you in your *dwe*lling
to see your strength and glory.
For your love is better than *life*,
my lips will speak your praise.
Response
So I will bless you all my *life*,
in your name I lift up my hands.
My soul shall be filled as with a *ban*quet,
my mouth shall praise you with joy.
Response

THE LORD IS KIND AND MERCIFUL

USE: *Petition*

The___ Lord is kind and mer-ci-ful.

TONE

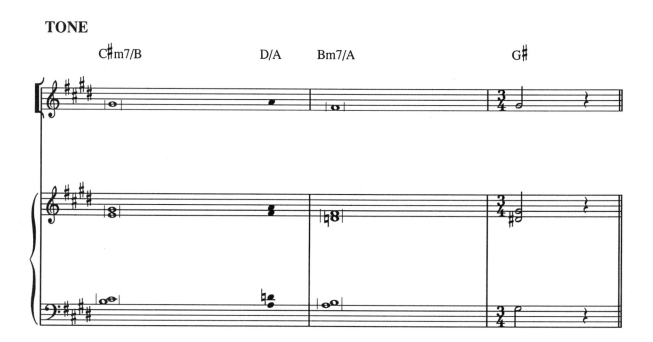

82

# PSALM OF PETITION 3 *The Lord's merciful kindness*

Psalm 138

I thank you, Lord, with all my *heart*,
you have heard the words of my <u>mouth</u>.
In the presence of the angels I will *bless* you.
I will adore before your holy <u>tem</u>ple.
> *Response*

I thank you for your faithfulness and *love*
which excel all we ever knew of <u>you</u>.
On the day I called, you *an*swered;
you increased the strength of my <u>soul</u>.
> *Response*

The Lord is high yet looks on the *low*ly;
and the haughty, God knows from a<u>far</u>.
Though I walk in the midst of af*flic*tion
you give me life and frustrate my <u>foes</u>.
> *Response*

Psalm 145

The Lord is kind and full of com*pas*sion,
slow to anger, abounding in <u>love</u>.
How good is the Lord to *all*,
compassionate to all cre<u>a</u>tion.
> *Response*

O Lord you are faithful in all your *words*
and loving in all your <u>deeds</u>.
You, O Lord, support all who *fall*
and raise up all who are bowed <u>down</u>.
> *Response*

You are just in all your *ways*
and loving in all your <u>deeds</u>.
You are close to all who *call* you,
who call on you from their <u>hearts</u>.
> *Response*

INSTRUMENTAL PARTS

Solo Instrument (flute, violin etc.)

Psalm 25   TO YOU, O LORD

ANTIPHON *Moderately*

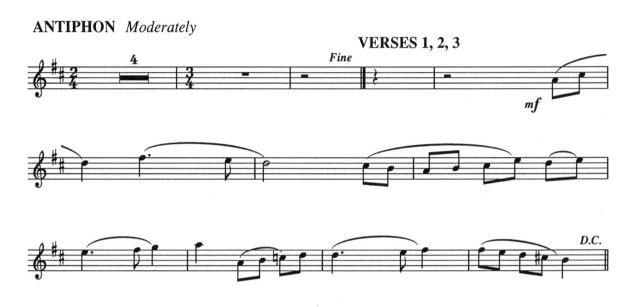

Psalm 51   BE MERCIFUL, O LORD

ANTIPHON *Slow with gentle pulse*

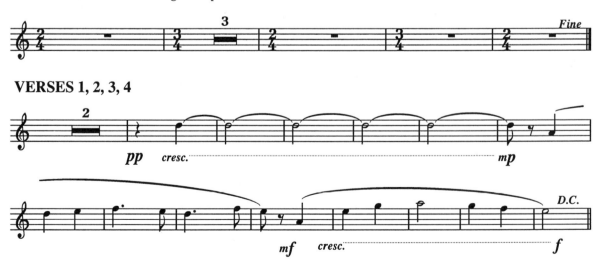

Psalm 27   THE LORD IS MY LIGHT

ANTIPHON 1   *With a gentle movement*

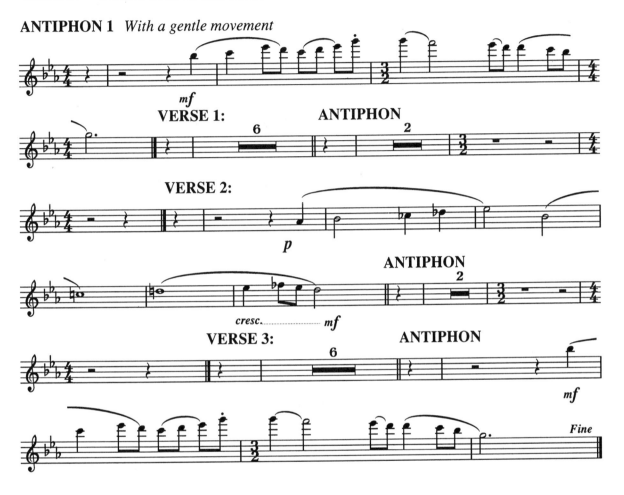

Psalm 103   THE LORD IS KIND AND MERCIFUL

ANTIPHON   *Expressively*

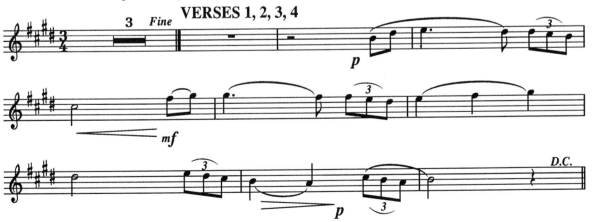

PERFORMANCE NOTES

Common Responsorial Psalms

In general, these psalm settings should be performed in this manner: the accompanying instrument, or group of instruments, first plays the antiphon as an introduction, unless a specific introduction appears in the score. The cantor, or perhaps a small group in the choir, sings the antiphon which the assembly is then invited to repeat. Thereafter, the cantor/choir sings the verses and the people respond at the end of each verse with the antiphon. Where an antiphon is set in parts for the choir, the vocal harmony might best be kept until the melody of the antiphon is well established in the assembly.

Ps 25   To you, O Lord
The verses should be delivered smoothly and evenly. A part for flute, or other soprano instrument, is provided to accompany the verses.

Ps 85   Lord, let us see your kindness
The phrase, "I will hear what the Lord God has to say", precedes the first verse only. Each verse should build slightly as it proceeds.

Ps 98   All the ends of the earth
A choice of two antiphons is given. Verse 5 of the psalm modulates from the key of G to A flat. Because of this change of key and the awkwardness this may present some instrumentalists, the capo chord symbols are given only as far as verse 4. The final antiphon has an optional descant for the second antiphon.

Ps 72   Lord, every nation
A strong metric pulse should govern this psalm. The pattern for Verse 3 varies somewhat from that of the other verses.

Ps 51   Be merciful, O Lord
A simple delivery will best convey the beauty of these words. An instrumental obbligato is provided for the verses.

Ps 91   Be with me, Lord
The expression in the Antiphon should be warm with smooth phrasing in the vocal parts. The Verses are more declamatory.

Ps 130 With the Lord there is mercy
The Antiphon should be sung simply while the words of the verses be sung expressively and with tonal colour.

Ps 22   My God, my God
This psalm should move at a measured pace and with simple expression.

Ps 136 God's love is everlasting

A small group in the choir (schola) sings the short refrain, "God's love is everlasting", after each line of the cantor's verses. After three such lines the assembly responds with the full Antiphon. The music should grow as it progresses.

Ps 118 This is the day

Keep all the quavers at constant value: no group forms triplets.

Ps 66 Let all the earth

Be careful of the rhythm in the third and seventh bars of the Antiphon; the quaver beat remains constant.

Ps 47 God mounts the throne

Play the short introduction before each repetition of the Antiphon. Keep the momentum of the verses steady.

Ps 104 Lord, send out your Spirit

Keep the transition from Antiphon to Verse steady: one bar of the Antiphon equals one crotchet beat in the Verse. The instrumental link is played each time after the Antiphon. The first Verse is sung by the Cantor; Verse 2 by two equal voices, or two groups of equal voices: Verse 3 by the full choir. All three Verses may, of course, be sung by Cantor alone.

Ps 19 Lord, you have the words

The Verses should not be hurried, and may go at an even slower pace than the Antiphon.

Ps 27 The Lord is my light

A choice of two Antiphons is given for this psalm. The Verses offer a variety of textures and harmonies for communities that have a cantor and choir. Like all these settings, however, it is possible for a cantor alone to sing the Verses without choral support. For the second Antiphon, a version with descant is given that may be sung after the last Verse. An instrumental obbligato is provided for the first Antiphon and its Verses.

Ps 34 Taste and see

The psalm calls for a simplicity of expression.

Ps 63 My soul is thirsting

The Verses should not be rushed.

Ps 95 If today you hear God's voice

The music depends for its effectiveness upon rhythmic crispness and clear diction. Verses 1 and 2 conclude with an optional line for equal voices. Verse 3 is written throughout for equal voices. Another possibility for four-part choirs singing this verse is to have the women's voices sing the equal voice version and the men's voices sing the melody line down an octave.

Ps 100 **We are God's people**
Only Verses 1, 2 and 4 of this psalm are given in the Lectionary. Verse 3 also has been set here to provide the complete psalm. The inclusion of Verse 3 would make the psalm suitable as an opening song. Choose a speed that avoids making the Verses sound rushed. Once the Antiphon is established, it may be sung in canon at a bar's distance.

Ps 103 **The Lord is kind and merciful**
The text and setting of this Antiphon are the same as the last of the Common Responses. An unforced expression will work best in the Verses. An instrumental part is provided to accompany the Cantor in the Verses.

Ps 145 **I will praise your name**
The second half of each Verse should not be hurried, particularly over the triplets.

Ps 122 **Let us go rejoicing**
The music should move with an even tread. The pattern for Verse 1 differs slightly from that of the other Verses.

Common Responses
The setting of the Response and its accompanying psalm Tone appears on the left-hand side of the book. On the facing page are printed a couple of *sample* psalm texts pointed to be sung to the Tone. The syllable in italics indicates when one moves from the reciting note to the cadential note mid-way through the Tone; the underlined syllable indicates the final cadential note. Each cadence always falls on an accented syllable. Depending on the text, a Tone may be sung *once* or *twice* between recurrences of the Response.

About the Composer

CHRIS WILLCOCK

Christopher Willcock is a member of the Jesuit Community, Parkville, Melbourne. A specialist in music and liturgy, his music is sung in churches in several countries.

As a musician, Father Willcock has been involved in choral direction in Australia; has undertaken a number of commissions for groups such as The Melbourne Chorale and the International Commission on English in the Liturgy (ICEL); and directed and organised two multi-media presentations, *Rejoice in the Word* (1984) and *Let there be Light* (1985), staged at the Sydney Opera House and the Melbourne Concert Hall.

Father Willcock is involved in teaching courses in Sacraments and Liturgical studies to theology students. He has studied music at the Conservatorium in Sydney and he holds a Doctorate in Theology from the Institut Catholique, Paris.

Currently a member of the ICEL Psalter sub-committee, Father Willcock's other publications include *Songs of Prayer*, *Trocaire* and *God of Peace* – all published by Collins Dove, Melbourne.